Backyard Chickens

The Essential Backyard Chickens Guide for Beginners: Choosing the Right Breed, Raising Chickens, Feeding, Care, and Troubleshooting

Andy Jacobson

Contents

Foreword

Chickens are the obvious livestock choice if you are planning to take a plunge into a self-sufficient homesteading lifestyle. Chickens don't require much space and they make little noise compared to other livestock animals. This means that they can easily be raised in both the rural and urban setting. On top of this, chickens require a modest amount of care and purchasing young chicks or fertilized eggs is very affordable.

Raising and breeding chickens is an incredibly rewarding hobby and all you need is the right guidance to get you started - this is exactly what this essential guide provides. You will learn how to choose the right breed, the things you need to consider before committing to keeping backyard chickens, how to purchase and raise baby chicks, how to purchase and start with adult birds, and everything you need to consider when selecting or designing your chicken coop.

By the end of this guide you will know how to:

- Purchase your birds, what to look for when purchasing your birds, how many to purchase and what gender.
- Raise chickens in any backyard.
- House your chickens.
- Feed and care for your flock.
- Raise baby chicks.
- Prevent and control pests.

- Protect your flock from predators.
- Prevent and deal with internal and external parasites.
- And much more!

This guide includes photos with clear explanations to further your understanding. Not only will you be introduced to the essentials of raising chickens, but I will also share with you the challenges that many initially face, and how to overcome them. If you are new to raising backyard chickens, I recommend going through this book in the order it has been structured with. This will put you on a steady path to raising a happy and productive flock that will bring you great satisfaction for years to come!

Best wishes,

Andy Jacobson

Section 1: Why Raise Chickens?

Increasing amounts of people today are keeping backyard chickens and there are many good reasons for this. Before delving into the essentials of backyard chicken raising, we will briefly outline the pros and cons of keeping chickens.

Improved Nutrition and Great-Tasting Eggs

As the saying goes, 'you are what you eat.' Having a constant supply of fresh eggs is certainly an amazing reason to raise chickens. More importantly however, chickens in traditional farming are fed a chemically engineered and antibiotic laden diet. Free range eggs from backyard chickens are much richer in nutritional value. They are said to contain seven times the amount of Vitamin A and double the amount of Vitamin E, on top of much greater amounts of Omega 3 and Beta Carotene and a lower amount of saturated fats. Compared to commercially produced chicken meat which are raised on antibiotics, arsenic, grains, and garbage, meat from backyard chickens is substantially better for your health and also significantly more flavorsome.

Animal Welfare

Beyond the health factors are of course concerns regarding animal welfare. You will have the satisfaction of knowing that your chickens are living a natural and comfortable life. Additionally, you will not be financially supporting factory-farming industries and their cruel practices which are not only harming the animals, but also our human health environment.

Public Health

Due to the extreme crowding and poor hygiene conditions, many corporate factory farms are breeding grounds for salmonella and E. coli which can then be passed onto humans through eggs, dairy, and meat. To combat these risks and to make the chickens grow faster, factory chickens are usually fed with antibiotics and other chemicals. Research has shown that the overuse of antibiotics in factory farming has led to an evolution of antibiotic-resistant bacteria that continues to threaten public health and compromise quality of life.

Environmental Health

Industrial agriculture is known to be among the leading causes of water pollution and one of the heaviest contributors of greenhouse gases. Keeping backyard chickens on the other hand, helps us decrease our carbon footprint. Firstly, raising chickens locally and sustainably does help reduce organic waste which would otherwise go into landfills and turned into methane gases. Instead of burning chicken manure, it can be recycled and used as an efficient fertilizer for your garden! On top of this, your chickens will help you cut down your food waste - they love to eat leftover fruits, vegetables and table scraps.

Organic Weed and Pest Control

Chickens also love eating a range of insects and weeds. Keeping chickens therefore provides you with a completely free and organic method for pest and weed control! Just make sure to fence off any vegetable beds that you may have in your garden to avoid your chickens from pecking at the vegetables on the ground.

Entertainment and Education

Chickens are inquisitive animals with unique personalities – they can be very entertaining. They might even inspire you to learn more about avian biology, sustainability, and animal welfare. On top of this, keeping backyard chickens will teach you valuable lessons of self-sufficiency, from having your own healthy source for eggs and meat to converting to organic sources of fertilizer, pest and weed control.

As with most things, there are also some downsides to keeping backyard chickens. These are however quickly outweighed by the above considerations. Firstly, an initial investment is required to purchase or construct a coop, run, and fencing. This is nevertheless outweighed by the long-term returns that you receive from keeping backyard chickens. Secondly, keeping chickens does require some time commitment and coop maintenance. You will need to make sure that your chickens have enough food, water and grit on a daily basis. The coop will also need cleaning and litter replacement a couple of times a year. Lastly, your chickens will also need protection from predators. You should therefore learn about the predators in your area and their behavior in order to ensure your flock is kept safe!

Overall, I hope you are assured that the pros strongly outweigh the cons and you are excited to progress onto the next steps of raising your own chickens.

Section 2: Choosing the Right Breed for You

There are many different breeds of chickens and different breeds have different characteristics. Which chicken breed is right for you will ultimately depend on your chicken raising goals. In this section, we will give you an overview of the most common chicken breeds in order to make it easier to choose the right breed for you.

Chicken Breeds

Chicken breeds are grouped into a number of different categories. Below is a list of the main three categories.

- **Egg-Layers:**
  Although these chickens can be eaten, they do not make good meat birds. Egg layers lay around 300 eggs in their first year and only slightly less in subsequent years.

- **Meat Breeds:**
  These breeds of chicken are not good egg-layers, but have been developed to grow fast and reach a larger frame.

- **Dual-Purpose Breeds:**
  These breeds are the most commonly kept breeds by homesteaders. They lay eggs relatively well and also make relatively good meat birds.

On top of the above categories, there are show breeds – chicken breeds which are kept for purely ornamental reasons – among many other categories. For the purpose of this guide however, we will be looking exclusively at the above three breed categories and the most commonly raised chicken types within each breed.

Dual-Purpose Breeds

Although you get fewer eggs overall and they grow slower compared to meat birds, dual-purpose breeds offer the best of both worlds for the casual chicken-keeper.

Barnevelders: The Barnevelder is a medium-heavy breed of chicken (6-7 lbs.) from northern Europe. They are calm and docile birds who are famous for their large chocolate brown eggs.

Type: Large Fowl, Bantam

Egg Facts:

- Egg production: Good, around 3 per week

- Egg color: Dark brown
- Egg size: Large

Suitability to Backyard Living:

- Confinement tolerance: Yes, handles confinement well
- Weather tolerance: Less cold hardy
- Behavior: Active, yet very docile and friendly
- Broodiness: No

Brahmas: Originally from India, the Brahma are big, heavy, and fluffy birds (8+ lbs.) with feathered legs. They mature slowly, but are very gentle and robust birds which are both cold and heat hardy.

Type: Large Fowl, Bantam

Egg Facts:

- Egg production: Good, around 3 per week
- Egg color: Brown
- Egg size: Medium

Suitability to Backyard Living:

- Confinement tolerance: Yes, tolerates confinement
- Weather tolerance: Robust, very hardy in heat and cold
- Behavior: Quiet and tame
- Broodiness: Yes

Orpingtons: The Orpington is a large and gentle breed of around 7-8 lbs. - originally from the United Kingdom. They lay brown eggs and are also very good mothers. They come in many different colors and are particularly rare in the black and blue varieties.

Type: Large Fowl, Bantam

Egg Facts:

- Egg production: Good, around 3 per week
- Egg color: Brown
- Egg size: Large

Suitability to Backyard Living:

- Confinement tolerance: Handles confinement well
- Weather tolerance: Very cold hardy
- Behavior: Docile birds who are also very calm and patient
- Broodiness: Yes

Wyandotte: The Wyandotte is an excellent meat bird that lays light to rich brown eggs. They are heavy and friendly birds (around 7-8 lbs.) who reach maturity moderately early. The Wyandotte, originally from North America, is often favored by backyard chicken-keepers because of their beautiful feather patterns.

Type: Large Fowl, Bantam

Egg Facts:

- Egg production: Very good, around 4 per week
- Egg color: Brown
- Egg size: Large

Suitability to Backyard Living:

- Confinement tolerance: Handles confinement well
- Weather tolerance: Robust and very cold hardy
- Behavior: Easygoing, but sometimes tend to become more aggressive
- Broodiness: Yes

Jersey Giants: As the name implies, the Jersey Giant is a giant from New Jersey. They are very heavy (8+ lbs.) and are the world's largest breed! Despite their size, they are not used commercially because they take relatively long to mature to full size (roughly 6 months).

Type: Large Fowl

Egg Facts:

- Egg production: Good, around 3 per week
- Egg color: Brown
- Egg size: X-Large

Suitability to Backyard Living:

- Confinement tolerance: Handles confinement well
- Weather tolerance: Robust, very cold hardy
- Behavior: Docile, good-natured and easy-going
- Broodiness: No

Australorps: The Australorp is an Australian dual-purpose bird that is an extremely good egg-layer. They are soft-feathered chickens who are very peaceful. If your intention is to keep a pet chicken, this is definitely a breed to consider!

Type: Large Fowl, Batnam

Egg Facts:

- Egg production: Excellent, around 5 per week
- Egg color: Brown
- Egg size: Large

Suitability to Backyard Living:

- Confinement tolerance: Handles confinement well
- Weather tolerance: Very hardy
- Behavior: Sweet, shy and peaceful
- Broodiness: Yes

Meat Birds

Cornish: The Cornish is a meat bird from Southwest England. Most commercial chickens are white Cornish X Rock hybrids. They are stocky (around 8+ lbs.) and mature quickly.

Type: Large Fowl, Bantam

Egg Facts:

- Egg production: Poor, around 1 per week

- Egg color: Light brown
- Egg size: small

Suitability to Backyard Living:

- Confinement tolerance: Tolerates confinement well
- Weather tolerance: Cold hardy
- Behavior: Docile and passive but quite noisy
- Broodiness: Yes

Both Wyandottes and Jersey Giants, although technically dual-purpose breeds, are also two of the main meat birds favored by homesteaders and small farmers. Wyandottes and Australorps are also amazing egg-layers. The next section covers the best egg-layers which are not dual-purpose.

The Best Egg-Layers

Rhode Island Reds: This American bird is the best breed for producing brown eggs. They are large and heavy (around 7-8 lbs) birds that are extremely hardy and make very good meat birds. Their valued meat and high laying productivity makes them very popular among small farmers and backyard homesteaders.

Type: Large Fowl, Bantam

Egg Facts:

- Egg production: Excellent, around 5 per week

- Egg color: Brown
- Egg size: X-Large

Suitability to Backyard Living:

- Confinement tolerance: Handles confinement well
- Weather tolerance: Hardy in heat and cold
- Behavior: Active, easy-going and fairly docile
- Broodiness: No

White Leghorns: These are ancient Mediterranean birds that are famous for their large white eggs. The White Leghorn is a medium-heavy breed of chicken (around 6-7 lbs.) who is active, intelligent, and tends to avoid human contact.

Type: Large Fowl, Bantam

Egg Facts:

- Egg production: Very good, around 4-5 per week
- Egg color: White
- Egg size: X-Large

Suitability to Backyard Living:

- Confinement tolerance: Handles confinement well
- Weather tolerance: Hardy and heat tolerant
- Behavior: Flighty, nervous but very tame
- Broodiness: No

Ameraucanas: The Ameraucana are rare and beautiful birds from South America who have muffs and a beard. They are very curious medium-heavy birds (around 6-7 lbs.) who lay eggs in different shades of blue and blue-green (not to be confused with Americanas who are Easter Eggers that can lay eggs in a variety of colors).

Type: Large Fowl, Bantam

Egg Facts:

- Egg production: Good, around 3 per week
- Egg color: Light blue, blue-green
- Egg size: Medium

Suitability to Backyard Living:

- Confinement tolerance: Handles confinement well
- Weather tolerance: Very cold hardy
- Behavior: Curious, sweet and mostly non-aggressive
- Broodiness: No

There are hundreds of chicken breeds currently in existence. We have covered the best and favorites in this section and hope that the above list has provided you with a general idea and knowledge to help you come to a decision. If you are after a rare or unusual bird, I encourage you to browse around. Using a range of online resources, you will find plenty of personal ratings on different chicken breeds from chicken-keepers around the world!

If you are not quite sure then it is firstly important to identify your priorities. To make your decision easier, try and answer the following questions which will help you determine which breed is right for you:

- Do you need a breed that is hardy in cold winters?
- Do you want a breed that will rear chicks?
- How important is egg-laying productivity to you?
- Do you want a breed that is docile and quiet?
- Do you want to have a colorful egg basket?

Before you go out and purchase chickens however, make sure to check with your zoning board to see whether there are any legal restrictions preventing you from keeping chickens in your backyard. Once you have received the green light, it's time to get started!

Section 3: Planning Ahead

There are many important decisions you need to make before becoming a chicken owner. The first which was covered in the previous section is deciding upon the right breed for you. Once you have made this decision, it is time to move onto the next important decisions. In this section, you will learn how to purchase your flock, what to look for, whether to buy chicks or chickens, male or female chickens, and the essentials of flock planning.

Eggs, Chicks, or Adult Birds?

There are three ways in which you can start raising chickens and it is for you to decide which of the following best suits your needs. For the absolute beginner, I would recommend starting with chicks: not only is it the most economical and practical way to start raising chickens, but seeing chicks grow to be adults is also a fascinating journey.

Starting with Fertile Eggs

There are several reasons why you may choose to hatch your own eggs instead of purchasing chicks or adult birds. Watching eggs hatch is an exciting and beautiful experience. You get to really connect with the life cycle of your chickens and you also get the opportunity to hatch rare breads and unusual colors.

Before purchasing fertile eggs of rare breeds however, it is advised to first practice your incubation technique. Incubation is tricky even with the best incubation equipment and you should never expect more than 50% of your eggs to hatch. How to go about hatching eggs is a topic that will be covered more closely in *Section 7* of this guide.

Lastly, it is important to keep in mind that you will have roosters in your flock if you decide to hatch eggs yourself. Eggs will usually hatch out in a 50:50 ratio of males and females. If you live in an urban setting, having roosters may be problematic: they are significantly louder than hens and keeping them is often against municipal regulations.

Hatching and incubation is a skill in itself. However, for beginners and those who don't want to invest in additional equipment for hatching and incubation, it is recommend that you start with either baby chicks or adult birds.

Male or Female Chickens?

Whether you need hens, roosters, or both will depend on your chicken-raising goals. If you are raising chickens that lay eggs, purchase either adult hens or female pullets (young hens) that have been sexed. Adult hens are more expensive but it will save you the waiting time. If your primary aim of keeping chicken is for meat, it is advised to order only cockerels (young males). Cockerels grow larger and faster than pullets and you generally won't have any problems with fighting unless you wait too long to butcher them.

It is important to keep in mind that hens do not need a rooster around to lay eggs and to live a normal life. If you live rurally and are not interested in breeding chickens, it might be a good idea to not keep a crowing rooster. Furthermore, if you intend to keep a small number of backyard chickens, it is not advised to have a rooster at all. For every rooster, there should be around 10 – 12 hens in your flock. If you do decide to keep roosters, there are a few considerations to be made:

- Make sure to choose the right breed for your backyard rooster. The breed will determine your rooster's temperament. The favorite breeds for roosters and multiple roosters include Brahmas, Orpingtons, Silkies (ornamental birds), Plymouth Rocks, Marans, and Australorps.
- Make sure that you have a plenty of running space and a couple of safe places to separate someone from the flock if necessary.
- If you plan to keep multiple roosters, it is advisable to raise them together in your flock. This way, they will establish a natural pecking order between them as

them grow up which will ensure peace in your backyard!

How Many?

It is important to note that chickens are social creatures and therefore it's crucial that you purchase at least two chickens to keep them happy. How many chickens you can ultimately raise will depend on your space, the size of your chicken coop, as well as local rules and regulations that sometimes limit the amount of chickens you can keep.

When deciding on how many chickens to keep, there are two primary considerations: space and eggs. The number of birds you wish to keep will also depend on your needs. If you have chosen chickens from a good laying breed, you can expect to receive 5-6 eggs per week. If your hens are not from an egg-laying strain, you can still expect to receive 2-3 eggs per week per hen. The size of your chicken coop will also determine the size of the flock you can keep. There should be around 2 to 4 sq. feet of floor area in your coop for each, and at least 4 sq. feet of area in the outdoor run.

Section 4: Purchasing and Starting with Chicks

As mentioned earlier, starting your chicken-raising experience with baby chicks is the most economical and practical way, especially if you are a beginner. There are many reasons for this, which include the following:

- Most hatcheries will sex the chicks for you.
- Chicks are usually less expensive than adult birds.
- Chicks are less likely to carry parasites or disease compared to adult birds.

Despite this, there are certain disadvantages to starting with baby chicks. Chicks are fragile and need protection. They require a lot of attention and special brooding equipment to keep them warm and protected. They also need time to mature and it will take at least 5 months or sometimes longer before female chicks mature to a stage where they start laying eggs. On top of this, it is important to keep in mind that the younger the chick, the harder it is to determine sex. While some hatcheries do a pretty good job in sexing chicks, mistakes do sometimes occur. It is also difficult to judge the quality of newly hatched chicks and you are therefore left with some ambiguity in terms of the sex as well as the quality of your chick.

You will also find that some hatcheries will offer 'starter birds'. These are older birds that are easier to sex, take less time to mature, and you will also have a better idea as to their quality. The cost of shipping starter birds is usually greater as they require special handling and it is also important to bear in mind that your choice in terms of breed selection will be more limited with starter birds. If you do opt for starter birds, make sure to find out their age as this will determine whether or not you will need a breeder (see *Section 8* for more details).

The easiest time to purchase baby chicks is in the spring and the early summer. You can purchase chicks either through online hatcheries or from farm stores or local breeders.

Purchasing Mail-Order Chicks

The following is a list of to-dos and things to be aware of when purchasing mail-order chicks:

- When ordering chicks online, there is usually a minimum order of 25 chicks. This is because chicks need to be packed closely together in boxes to keep them warm during shipping.
- Try to order your chicks when the weather is mild in your area. This is because even through they are grouped together, baby chicks can overheat or become too cold during transit.
- Mail-order chicks are usually hatched on demand. This means that when you order your chicks, they will first stay in the incubator for around 21 days before they are shipped out to you.

- Baby chicks can survive for 2-3 days without food or water after hatching. Baby chicks are usually shipped the day after they hatch and usually reach you within 24 hours (by U.S. Mail).
- When choosing an online hatchery, try and choose one that does guarantee 24-hour delivery to your area. To ensure a happy arrival, it is best to keep the shipping time as short as possible.
- Do not order any extras – hatcheries will usually add one or two free chicks to cover any possible losses during shipping. Some hatcheries will guarantee safe arrival while others do not.
- When your chicks get delivered or when you go to the post office to collect them (this will depend on the hatcheries' courier), make sure to open the box and inspect them immediately.
- In the event that you have lost some chicks, make sure to inform the post office. If your hatchery guarantees safe arrival, you can fill out a claims form and receive a refund or a replacement. Make sure to count your chicks before filing a claim as some hatcheries will add extra chicks to your order to account for any possible losses.

From a Local Breeder

Depending on where you live, you might also have the opportunity to purchase chicks from a local breeder. There are advantages and disadvantages of acquiring your chicks this way. Visiting your local breeder is usually an exciting and fun experience and you also get to speak to them directly to get some help and advice. You can build a relationship with your chicks straight away and you will also get a chance to see whether they look healthy and happy, which is a key advantage. On the other hand, breeders will rarely be able to vaccinate chicks against diseases. Furthermore, chick sexing is a specialist skill – it is possible that your local breeder won't be able to tell you what sex the chicks are.

From a Farm Store

You may also be able to purchase some chicks from a local farm store. Some farm stores take orders and some will only sell chicks in the spring. A great upside is that you can usually order less than 25 which is ideal for those with a small backyard coop. Some farm stores will also have some chicks to be bought on the spot. Ask around to see whether anyone knows what breed or sex the chicks are. If you are unsure about the information you receive, ask the person exactly how they know what sex the chick is. Bear in mind that it is impossible to tell what sex a newly hatched chick is by simply looking at it. You can only know the sex of a newly hatched chick if the chick is from a sex-linked line. If the store has just bought mixed chicks, be cautious as there is a chance that they are all roosters, or not the type or breed of chicken that you are after.

What to Look For

If you are buying mail-order chicks from a hatchery, it is important to ensure that your chicks are from a certified pullorum-tested flock. Good breeders will already have their flock tested and vaccinated from any bird diseases. If possible, ask and invest to have your chicks vaccinated for Mareks disease.

If you are buying your chicks directly from a store or breeder, look out for the following:

1. <u>Chick Sex:</u>

Remember, unless your chicks are sex-linked, it is impossible to tell whether they are female or male. Sex-linked chicks are hybrid chicks from two different breeds: the males will be one color and female chicks will be a different color.

Nevertheless, it is possible to determine a chick's sex a few days after hatching. This is done by looking inside the chick's vent area. Vent sexing is not easy and this is why hatcheries employ professional chicken sexers, which also explains why sexed chicks are more expensive. When purchasing chickens from a farm store or local breeder without the expertise, be prepared for surprises as your chick matures.

2. <u>Chick Health:</u>

The first step to having a healthy flock is by choosing healthy chicks! When purchasing your chicks, there are certain indicators by which you can judge the chick's health.

- **Movement** – Healthy chicks will sleep a lot but they are also very active when they get approached. It is not a good sign if a chick is touched but does not move. If a chick is panting or breathing quickly with the beak open, this either means that it is too warm or sick.

- **Noise** – Healthy chicks are generally active but quiet. If the chicks are noisy, this is usually a sign that they are stressed or there is another underlying problem. Noise is also an indication that they are cold, hungry, or thirsty. You can usually tell whether your the chicks are too hot or too cold. If they are too cold, they will be piled up together near the heat source. If they are too hot, they will be as far away from the heat source as possible. If the chicks are still noisy even though they have been fed and the temperature seems to be right, then something else is wrong. Avoid purchasing chicks when you are unsure of what is wrong with them. If you receive your chicks by mail, they will arrive active and noisy. However, after placing them in the right temperature with food and water they will quickly calm down!

- **Looks** – Healthy baby chicks will be clean, with no blood stains or feces attached to them, with bright and clear eyes. Some newly hatched chicks will have a very slight lump on their abdominal area which is normal. This is where the egg yolk used to be and as long as the area does not look red or sore, all is good! Their beaks and toes should be straight (not twisted or bent to the side). Note however that some hatcheries will trim the beaks of chicks to avoid them picking at one another. This is not a cause for concern.

3. Chick Color:

The color of your chicks can give you an idea as to whether you have the right chicks. If the color seems off, check whether you have received a substitute breed. You will usually receive a notification if you receive a substitute chick.

Chick color can vary from breed to breed and variations may even exist among chicks of the same breed. However, as a general rule of thumb:

- Dark chickens will have generally gray, brown and black chicks.
- Multicolored chickens whose feathers have patches or streaks will generally have yellow or brown chicks with faint dark stripes.
- White, buff and red chickens will generally have yellow chicks.

Other ways to determine breed include the following:

- Chicken breeds with crests and topknots have chicks that sometimes already have a slight topknot or puffy bump on the head.
- Chicken breeds with muffs and beards will have chicks that sometimes already have very slight muffs and beards.
- The color of the chick's leg should already be the same as the characteristic leg color of the breed.

Feather-footed chickens will have some chicks with regular legs that are indistinguishable from other chicks and some chicks that already have fluff growing on their legs.

Section 5: Purchasing and Starting with Adult Birds

If you want to start egg production straight away and don't want to worry about raising chicks, you may wish to make the decision to purchase adult birds. You will also have a much better idea as to the quality and color of your bird when purchasing adult birds. There are however certain disadvantages that ought to be considered that are directly linked with age. Firstly, it is often hard to tell how old a chicken is once it is an adult. Older hens will usually lay fewer or no eggs and older roosters may no longer be fertile. Secondly, older birds are significantly more likely to have been exposed to parasites and/or diseases. Because of this, close examination is crucial to make sure you are purchasing a healthy flock.

Purchasing Adult Birds

Although adult birds can occasionally by purchased through mail order, shipping is usually expensive. Because of this, it is usually better to get adult chickens from a reputable breeder in your area.

What to Look for

It is always recommend going to see your chicken before committing to the purchase. This will allow you to see your chicken's home and also ask questions. At the very minimum, the breeder should be able to tell you the breed, sex, and age of of the chicken. The following is a list of things that you should look for and inquire about before committing to purchase.

1. **Chicken Health:**

When choosing your chicken from the hatchery, make sure that the chicken is active and alert and lives in a clean environment. They should not have any big bare patches, wounds, or sores. Note that hens may have a small bare patch at the back of the neck from mating, but this is not a cause for concern.

Generally speaking, a healthy chicken should show the following:

- Alert and active.
- Clean nostrils with no discharge.
- Bright and clear eyes. Runny eyes and nasal discharge are both signs of illness.
- Breathe with the beaks shut. A healthy chicken will not be breathing with an open beak unless it is very hot.
- The comb (the fleshy growth at the top of their head) and the wattles (two oblong fleshy growths that hang below their chin) should be plump and glossy. In roosters, black patches of the comb can be an

indication of frostbite that can temporarily cause infertility.

- The feathers should be smooth with no big bare batches. Look through the feathers to make sure the chicken does not have lice.
- The legs are smooth with shiny skin and four or five toes depending on the breed.
- There should be no swellings or lumps on the body or on the bottom of the feet.

2. Chicken Age:

Determining the sex of an adult chicken is straightforward. The feathers, features, and coloring will differ significantly. Roosters crow and will have longer tail feathers, a larger comb and larger wattles. On the other hand, determining the age of the chicken is more difficult.

A chicken's life span is about 8 years. Roosters are only fertile for about 3 years and hens only lay well for around 3 years. To avoid buying an unproductive bird, it is therefore incredibly important to determine the chicken's age.

It can be difficult to tell the age of the chicken once fully matured but the following are a few indicators that will give you a general idea:

- Old chickens will have thick, dry and flaky skin on the legs. Younger chickens will have smooth shanks.
- The easiest way to tell the age of a rooster is by looking at the length of his spur (the horn-like protrusion that grows on their legs). The older the rooster, the longer the spur. Something to be aware of is that spurs are sometimes removed.
- Hens that stop laying will also develop longer spurs.
- Hens that are laying eggs will have combs and wattles that are deep red in color, glossy and moist-looking. Older hens (and older roosters as well) will have duller and dryer combs and wattles.
- Hens that are laying have a widely spaced pubic bone with a large and moist cloaca. Older hens that no longer lay eggs will have a narrower pubic bone and the cloaca will appear shriveled and smaller in size.

3. <u>Other Things to Consider:</u>

You may also want to check a rooster's temperament by going inside the coop and seeing whether he acts aggressively. It is generally recommended to avoid an aggressive rooster, especially when you are a beginner – they can also be dangerous to have around children.

It is important to note that if you are going to see chickens in the fall, which is generally not recommended, they might look scruffy from molting. Molting is when a chicken looses feathers to replace them. This is usually a bad time to purchase chickens as it will be difficult to gauge their health. During this time, chickens are also more prone to illness which can be triggered from a change in environment or shipping.

Lastly, if you are looking to purchase a show bird, it is important to familiarize yourself with the qualification for the specific chicken breed you are after before purchasing your bird. The American Poultry Association publishes a book every few years outlining breed standards.

Taking Your Chickens Home

When visiting a breeder to purchase your chickens to take home, make sure to bring a proper carrier. A standard pet carrier will suffice, although you can buy carriers that are specifically designed for chickens. Make sure that there is enough room in the carrier for your chickens to stand up, lie down, and turn around. Carriers should also have good ventilation. It is also important to be watchful of temperature to make sure your chickens don't overheat. If the trip home takes longer than 12 hours, it is important to clip a water container to the carrier.

Section 6: Chicken Coops – Everything You Need

Whether you decide to buy or build your own chicken coop, there are a few key criteria that need to be fulfilled to ensure that your flock remains healthy and safe!

Coop Size

- Generally speaking, small sized chickens (Bantam chickens) need at least 1 to 2 square feet of indoor space per bird and around 4 to 6 square feed of outdoor running space per bird.
- Medium sized chickens (laying chickens) need need at least 2 square feet of indoor space per bird and around 8 square feed of outdoor running space per bird.
- Large chickens require at least 2 square feet of indoor coop space per bird and 10 square feed of outside running space per bird.

Protection from Predators

Chickens need to be protected from potential predators, particularly during the night when they are most vulnerable. Make sure that your flock is sheltered from predators from above, below, and from the sides. If your coop does not have a floor, it is important to bury some small-mesh fencing roughly 12 inches below the ground of your coop to protect your flock from rodents. The side fencing of your coop should also be buried around 12 inches into the ground. This will prevent sneaky predators from digging their way into the chicken coop.

Ventilation

Your chicken coop will require good ventilation. Sufficient ventilation can be provided through windows, exhaust fans, roof vents and through other means. If your chicken coop is particularly tall, it will require ventilation both near the top and near the bottom of the coop. If your coop is not so tall, ventilation from the top is preferred because this allows for ventilation without drafts. The coop needs to have a good airflow which will prevent your flock from developing respiratory diseases. At the same time, make sure to insulate any drafty spots particularly during the colder months.

Clean, Warm and Dry Shelter

To ensure your flock remains healthy, the coop has to be warm and dry. The most comfortable temperature for backyard chickens is anything between 40 to 85 degrees Fahrenheit. Make sure that your chicken coop is well designed and suited to your climate. Chickens should be protected from any cool drafts and winter winds as they cannot withstand the cold for too long. If your chickens are raised in a hot climate, make sure to provide extra space, high ceilings and very good ventilation. Lastly, it is crucial to keep the coop clean in order to avoid parasite infestation, odor or moisture build-up.

Other Elements

- **Droppings tray:** To help keep the coop clean, it is recommended to place a removal tray below the roosting poles. This will allow you to easily dispose of any droppings and easily collect fertilizer for your garden.
- **Feeder and water station:** You should also provide a feeder and a water station. These should hang around 7 inches off the ground.
- **Lighting:** Providing light is crucial for your chickens' health. Chickens need light to eat, drink and to lay eggs. An artificial light during the winter makes sure they remain active and also protects them from predators.
- **Nesting boxes:** Nesting boxes should be raised a few inches above the ground but below the lowest rooster. Layers can share nesting boxes but you should provide at least 1 next box for every four to five chickens. They should be at least 12 x 12 inches in size and contain around 1 – 2 inches of nesting material, such as wood shavings.
- **Roosts:** You should also provide roosting poles for your birds to sleep on. Allow around 5 – 10 inches of space per bird.

Proper housing is key for your chicken's happiness! You will need your chicken coop to be durable, sturdy, and predator-proof. Investing in a good coop, whether you build it yourself or purchase a pre-assembled coop, is a long-term investment for your chickens. It is essential to their health and safety!

Section 7: Feeding Your Flock

Chickens are scavengers and will actively search and hunt for food. Because chickens don't have a strong sense of taste, they will eat almost anything! But just eating anything will generally not satisfy their nutritional needs and therefore it is important for the chicken-keeper to control and guide their food choices. Providing your chickens with a healthy and balanced diet will also ensure that they remain healthy and provide an abundance of nutritious eggs for you.

1. _Choosing the Best Feed for Your Flock_

Depending on the type and age of your chickens, they will need need around 16 – 24% of quality protein. They will also need some fat, carbohydrates, vitamins and minerals. Whilst you can feed your flock homemade food, this is not recommended for a number of reasons. Firstly, homemade food is not cheaper than commercially purchased feed. In fact, purchasing the grains individually will cost more and is also very time-consuming. More importantly, making your own chicken feed requires a complex understanding of chicken nutrition. The nutritional requirements of chickens also vary greatly depending on their age and the type of chicken. This is why companies hire experts that test different feeds which are tailored specifically to your chicken's needs.

You have likely heard that some people let their flock feed on pasture. However, even if your chickens have unrestricted access to large pieces of land, they will not be able to get the right amount of feed with the right amount of nutrients unless you supplement their pasture with other nutrient-rich feed.

The most efficient way to provide a healthy and balanced diet for you flock is therefore to purchase complete commercial rations from a feed store. When purchasing complete rations, you will need to make sure to get the correct feed for the type and age of chickens you want to feed.

Choosing the Right Feed

A good quality chicken feed should be the mainstay for your flock's diet. To pick the best feed for your chickens it is important to understand the purpose of the different feeds that are available.

Most all-purpose poultry feed will not be designed for your egg-layers or meat birds. Commercial feed will have labels that indicate the age and the type of chicken the feed is designed for.

Starter Rations for Baby Chicks

There are different starter rations. If your chicks are layers, they will need a feed called 'starter feed' or 'chicken starter' which should contain about 20% protein. Meat chicks on the other hand, require a feed that is high in protein (around 22 – 24%) for the first six weeks. These feeds are usually called 'broiler starter' or 'meat bird starter'.

Some people also choose to feed their chicks with medicated feed for the first few weeks. For the backyard chicken-keeper, feeding your clock medicated feed is not completely necessary. If you do however choose to do so, it is worth noting that one bag of medicated feed should suffice and that you should continue feeding them with un-medicated feed thereafter. For layers, it is recommended to stop using medicated feed at 18 weeks and for meat birds you should stop using medicated feed at least 2 weeks before the butchering date. This is to ensure that none of the medication ends up in the eggs or the meat intended for human consumption.

Rations for Your Egg-Layers

If you are raising egg-layers, then you will have to purchase around three different types of feed depending on the age of your flock.

1. **Grower Pullet Ration (week 6 – 14)**: Rations for growing pullets should be fed to your chickens from when they leave the brooder at 6 weeks until they are

about 14 weeks old. Growing pullet rations should have around 18% protein which, allowing your chickens to grow slowly enough that they can develop strong bones and a healthy body in preparation for egg production.

2. **'Developer Pullet Ration' or 'Finishing Pullet Ration' (week 15 – 22):** From week 15 until week 22 or until they start laying eggs, the protein intake of your layers should be reduced to about 16%. The feed should contain normal levels of vitamins and minerals. Feeding a diet that is high in calcium and phosphorus can harm the kidneys of young birds.

3. **Adult Layer Ration (from week 22 onwards):** Your hens will need a protein level of 16 to 18% once they reach 22 weeks or start laying eggs. Make sure to not feed adult layer rations to other types of chickens as the high mineral content can damage the kidneys of other birds.

For birds that are laying a large number of eggs, you can provide them with extra calcium. Commercially bought layer feed will usually already contain calcium supplements. But if your hens are laying eggs with thin or soft eggshells, this is an indication of calcium deficiencies in your birds. If required, dried eggshells that are ground to powder can provide an additional high calcium supplement. It is important not to force too much calcium onto your laying hens. You can provide them with extra calcium by crushing up oyster shells for example and adding these to the feeder. This way your hens can choose how much calcium to take in.

If you are breeding chickens, it is also advised to keep your hens on a laying ration. For roosters, protein intake should be increased.

Rations for Meat Birds

Backyard chicken-keepers will generally encounter two types of meat birds: The Cornish X Rock hybrid which grows very quickly, and the heritage or free-range meat birds that grow significantly slower.

Cornish X Rock broiler:

- These birds should be maintained on a 'broiler starter' or 'meat bird starter' feed for the first six weeks (20 – 24% protein).
- After six weeks and until they are butchered, the protein should be lowered to 18 – 20%. These rations are called 'finishing rations' or 'grower rations.' It is important to check that the feed does not contain any antibiotics because traces will otherwise be found in the meat.

Free-range heritage meat birds:

- These birds should be maintained on a 'broiler starter' or 'meat bird starter' feed for the first six weeks (20 – 24% protein).
- From week 6 to week 12, the protein can be lowered to 18 – 20%.
- From week 12 until they are butchered, the protein should be lowered to 16%.

Three Forms of Feed

There are three forms of feed that you can generally choose from: crumbles, pellets, and mash. Research has shown that crumbles are the best and preferred form of feed. Flocks that are fed crumbles appear to be happier, healthier, grow faster and lay more eggs. The second best feed form is pellets, which are commonly used for adult birds. Mash is the least preferred form of feed.

If mash is the only option open to you, you can add some warm water to the mash before feeding your chicken. Chickens usually prefer this. However, when feeding your chicken mash with water, make sure that the mixture is not left untouched too long as it can otherwise spoil and turn moldy – this can cause harm to your flock.

Always Check the Label!

It is always advised to double-check the label before purchasing commercial feed. In particular, look out for the following:

- **Manufactured date or expiration date:** Most feeds loose their nutrients and turn stale after around six months. While this will not directly harm your flock, it will not provide them with the vitamins and minerals they need which can in in the long term result in vitamin deficiencies.

- **Always check the ingredients:** Look at the protein, fat and vitamin percentage.

- **Check whether the feed contains medications:** Check if and what medications are included. If the feed contains medications, it is also important to check how long the chicken has to be off the feed before its eggs or meat can be consumed.

2. *Providing Water and Grit*

Besides a quality feed, it is important to provide your flock with a constant supply of grit to facilitate digestion. Grit can also be purchased it feed stores and it helps your chickens break down food particles. Make sure that the grit you're purchasing is designed for birds. Coarse shell grit is a good choice.

Having a source of clean and safe water is also very

important. In normal weather, one chicken will drink approximately a pint of water per day. They will drink nearly double this in hot weather conditions. Broilers also tend to drink more because they have a faster metabolism. It is essential to the health of your chicken that they are provided with unlimited water. Chickens with unrestricted access to clean water tend to lay more eggs, grow faster, and are significantly healthier.

Make sure that the water is clean and cool as chickens will avoid drinking dirty water and they dislike warm water. In hot weather, making sure there is a constant supply of cool water is essential to the wellbeing of your flock.

3. _Treating Your Flock_

In addition to a quality chicken feed, you can occasionally also treat your chickens with a variety of fresh fruit and vegetables.

When treating your flock, make sure to only give them as many treats as they can eat at any given time in order to keep pests away. As a general guidance on how many treats you can feed your chickens, a cup per chicken per week, spread over several days of the week, is a good amount. Make sure that the scraps you give to your chickens are not high in fat or salt. Avoid feeding any spoiled or rancid food.

The following is a list of some good and safe treats you can give your chickens. Make sure to provide treats in small quantities only and to clean up any treats they get eaten up.

Raw fruits and vegetables that can be fed include:

- Bok choy
- Cabbage
- Chickweed
- Endive
- Fruit, e.g. banana
- Silverbeet
- Spinach
- Vegetable peels

Table foods that can be fed occasionally include:

- Beans
- Bread
- Cooked pasta
- Legumes
- Rolled oats
- Wholemeal rice
- Grains, e.g. wheat and corn

4. _Things to Avoid Feeding Your Flock_

Here is a list of the things you should absolutely avoid

feeding your chickens.

Do not feed your chickens the following:

- Anything moldy. Moldy food can make chickens very sick.
- Avocado: Avocadoes contain a fatty acid called *persin* which can be fatal to birds.
- Chocolate: Chickens do not tolerate chocolate, especially dark chocolate.
- Citrus fruits or lawn mower clippings: These foods should be avoided because they tend to become moldy quickly.
- Green areas of potatoes: These should be avoided by humans and not fed to chickens because they are poisonous.
- Leaves from the following vegetables: tomato, pepper, potato, and eggplant.
- Onion and garlic.
- Raw dry beans: Some types of raw dried beans have toxins which are not safe for your chickens to eat. It is therefore advised to always cook your beans before feeding these to your chickens.
- Raw peanuts: These should be avoided because they contain a fungus called *aflatoxin* which your chickens won't tolerate.
- Rhubarb: Rhubarb leaves contain poisonous oxalic acid.
- The following garden plants should be avoided: sweat pea, datura, and morning glory.

5. *When and How Much to Feed Your Flock*

Most chicken-keepers fill the chicken feeders with enough food to last a couple of days. This way, your chickens can eat several times a day, as they would otherwise do in a wild natural setting. This feeding method can be used for all types of chickens.

Other chicken-keepers prefer to feed their chickens each day, usually once in the morning and once in the evening. This allows them to better control their chicken's diet, particularly if the chickens are too heavy. It also takes away feed that may otherwise attract pests. Overall, how you wish wish to feed your flock is a matter of preference.

How much feed your chickens need will depend on your chicken type, age, size, breed, how active they are and the weather. Dual-purpose breeds will usually need more feed than lighter layer breeds. Because they have access to range and pasture in the summer months, your flock will usually eat significantly more in the autumn and winter.

I personally recommend feeding your flock 'free choice,' that is leaving the feeder out at all times so your chickens can eat as much as they need. The worst mistake new chicken-keepers can make is not to provide their flock with sufficient food. If you feel like you are using more feed than you should, this may be an indication that pests are eating it up during the night. If you are raising egg-layers, you can remove the feeder at night and put it out during daylight hours. If you are raising meat birds that must be fed day and night, you can put the feed inside a pest-proof container. Also make sure to provide a night-light for your meat birds - chickens don't like eating in the dark.

6. *Some Final Feeding Considerations*

When feeding your chickens, it is a good idea to occasionally watch them to make sure that the bigger birds are not excluding the younger and weaker birds. If you notice this sort of behavior, you should arrange to have them fed separately. If you notice any significant changes in the feeding behavior of your flock, it is always advised to consult a veterinarian.

For free-range hens, a weed lawn is recommended. Your flock should ideally also be given access to leaf litter and compost that contains earthworms and other burrowing insects.

Section 8: Raising Baby Chicks

Chicks need food, water, warmth and protection to thrive. There are two ways in which you can keep your chicks warm and protected. You can either place them in a brooder or you can help your hen provide warmth and protection. Both of these options will be discussed in this section.

If you already have a hen that is motherly and of a broody breed (see criteria as outlined in *Section 2* of this guide), you can, with a little help, have her take care of the chicks. If you have other older birds, it is advised to enclose the mothering hen and chicks in a cage to avoid any problems with the other chickens. Keep them enclosed until the chicks are approximately 3 months old. Your hen will provide warmth and protection. The feeding, watering and growing process which is the same whether or not chickens are raised in the brooder or with a hen, will be discussed in subsections 2 and 3.

1. _Brooders: Raising Chicks in a Brooder_

Chicks will need to be transferred from the incubator straight into the brooder. If your chicks are arriving via mail order or through a different source, it is advised to set up the brooder before they arrive. Upon arrival, they should immediately be placed inside the brooder. Chicks will need to be kept inside the brooder for around a month and potentially longer if the weather remains cool.

Brooder Specifications

The following are criteria which you should take into account in order to select the right breeder for your chicks:

- A standard chick will need around 6 square inches of space inside the brooder for the first month.

- Brooders need to be at least 18 inches deep. This is particularly important if the heat source is above the brooder.
- It is recommended that the brooder has a cover to prevent chicks from escaping. Deeper brooders will also prevent larger chicks from jumping out and escaping.
- The brooder should allow chicks to move from one 'warmer area' near the light source to a 'cooler area' further away from the light source so that they can find the right temperature that makes the comfortable. Rectangular brooder boxes allow for the heat source to be on one end and the cooler region to be on the other. Alternatively, if your brooder is round or square, the heat source should be in the center, allowing your chicks to move to the edge of the brooder should they get too warm.

The Perfect Temperature

For the first week inside the brooder, chicks should be kept at an ideal temperature of 95 degrees °F. This temperature should be measured at the chick's mid-height which will be around 2 inches off the ground.

You should lower this temperature by 5 degrees °F every week until you reach 70 degrees °F. During nighttime, it is important to ensure that the temperature does not fall below 60 degrees °F. For the first three months of your chicks' lives, the night temperature inside the brooder should be kept at

60 degrees °F.

When heating the brooder, it is important to make sure that you also provide good ventilation. If you are doubtful about whether air flow is sufficient and if the temperature inside the brooder keeps getting too hot, it is advised to drill a few small holes on the sides of the brooder. These holes should be made a few inches above the brooder floor, in order to facilitate cool airflow.

To determine temperature inside the brooder, and particularly if this is your first time raising chickens, it is recommended that you purchase a brooder thermometer for peace of mind – you can monitor it regularly. However, you do not necessarily need a thermometer as you can simply adjust the temperature according to the behavior of your chicks. It is possible and generally straightforward to tell whether temperature is optimal by simply observing your chicks and their body language. The following are a few useful indications:

- Chicks are generally active, yet quiet. If they are noisy, this is an indication that they are either hungry, thirsty, too hot or too cold.
- If your chicks are wandering around happily, some sleeping near the heat source, others eating and

drinking, then this is an indication that the temperature is ideal.

- If your chicks are bundled together near the heat source, then this is an indication that it's probably too cold. Chicks that are too cold will also eat less and be less active.
- If your chicks are panting with their beaks open and are huddled away from the heat source, then this is an indication that it's too hot inside the brooder. Chicks that are too hot will eat less, drink more, and are also less active.

Brooder Lighting

An incandescent light bulb attached to a fixture with a reflector can be used to raise 25 – 50 chicks. These bulbs are the least expensive heat source for raising chickens. Hanging over the brooder, the heat can be adjusted in to ways. You can either lower or increase the wattage of the bulb or you can raise or lower the fixture. Depending on the number of chicks you plan to raise, it is recommended to start with either a 60 or 100-watt bulb. Depending on the size of your brooder, it might also be a good idea to have two bulbs attached to the fixture in the event that one burns out in your absence causing the temperature to drop.

Alternatively, a 250-watt infrared heat lamp can be used to raise 25 – 100 chicks. These red lamps are generally more expensive but they don't burn out as quickly when compared to white lamps. Red lamps also discourage picking between the chicks. It is advised to use infrared heat lamps with caution as they can get quite hot, especially if you have a small brooder. Because of this, it is also absolutely crucial that the lamp has a porcelain socket and not a plastic one that could possibly melt. When using a 250-watt infrared lamp, hang the lamp 18 inches above the chickens. Raise the lamp further every week in order to reduce the heat. The lamp should be raised by 3 inches every week as your chicks grow. As your chickens get older, it is important to give them more room to move and so that they can also move away from the heat if they get too hot. Alternatively, you can also switch from an infrared heat lamp to incandescent lighting as they get older and require less heat.

Another lighting option, which is also the most expensive but the safest alternative, is to use to an Infratherm heating panel. Infratherm heating panels only heat the area directly below them which allow the chicks to move away into a cooler area more easily. The panels also use significantly less electricity and are therefore more cost-efficient in the long-term. If you are thinking about keeping chickens for a couple of years, and raising chicks regularly, I strongly recommend making this investment which will pay for itself over time.

When transferring your chicks into the brooder, it is recommended to light the brooder continuously for the first 48 hours. However, during this time, it is advised to train your chicks to tolerate darkness. It is therefore advised to turn off the light for a short time (30 minutes maximum) once or twice a day during the first 24 hours so that they slowly get familiar with darkness. Another option is to use a dim light. If you are raising egg-layers, then it will usually suffice to keep the light on for 12 hours a day. For broiler chicks however, the light has to be on for 24 hours a day because chicks do not eat in the dark, and in order to sustain their growth, chicks will need to eat both during day and during night.

Brooder Set-Up

Besides enough space, a heat and a light source, starter rations and an unrestricted supply of clean water, you will also need to provide your chicks with bedding. This bedding will reduce the odor inside the brooder, dry any droppings as well as absorb any moisture.

The following are materials which are well-suited for bedding:

- Clean sand
- Coarse sawdust
- Grit, e.g. chick grit
- Pine shavings

You should **never** use the following for bedding:

- Paper, e.g. newspaper
- Cardboard
- Plastic on the bottom of the brooder, which can cause your chicks to develop splay legs (i.e. deformities of the leg)
- Cat litter
- Soil
- Vermiculite
- Perlite
- Cedar shavings
- Cotton batting
- Hay, straw or leaves, as well as any other material than can get moldy
- Hardwood shavings or other wood shavings, which can develop mold that can harm your chicks

Change the bedding completely whenever the it appears to

be damp or smelly. If the bedding is dirty-looking but still dry, it will usually suffice to just add an extra layer. When cleaning the brooder, remove the chicks and place them into a large box. Scrub the brooder with disinfectant, rinse and dry it before adding the bedding and your chicks.

To sum up therefore, the breeder should comprise of:

1. 6 square inches of space per chick
2. A heat and light source
3. Sufficient ventilation / air flow
4. Feeder with starter rations
5. Clean water source with cool water
6. Moisture-absorbing bedding

If you provide all this, your chicks will grow to be strong and healthy. We will cover the stages of growth of baby chicks in subsection 3 once we have discussed how to feed your chicks.

Transferring Your Chicks into the Brooder

To transfer the chicks into the brooder, remove them from their shipping container once at a time. Hold each chick close to the water source and gently dip their beak in the water for a short amount of time. Your chicks will be dehydrated from the journey and 'dipping beaks' will encourage them to drink. If one of your chicks appears to be particularly weak, try and drop one or two little drops of warm water into its beak, gently place it near the heat source, and hope for the best.

Do not worry if you encounter one or two dead chicks during the first few days. This is fairly common. Make sure to remove and bury dead chicks immediately.

Cover the bedding of the brooder with some paper for the first one or two days. Use paper with a rough surface or other textured paper to cover any loose bedding. This will prevent your chicks from eating too much of it. For the first few days, it is important to keep your chicks as undisturbed as possible. They will still be stressed from the journey need time to adapt and get used to their new environment. Just make sure that they have sufficient water and feed at all times. On the second day it is important to remove the paper from the bedding as this surface, as explained earlier, can lead to leg deformities as the chicks grow up.

It is important to observe and check up on your chicks as they grow. Make sure that they are eating and drinking and always check to see whether the temperature is right. If you spot any problems that cannot be solved by providing food and water or by adjusting the temperature, then it is important to contact the seller and inform them that you are having problems. The following are a few precautions which you should also take in order to ensure your chicks grow to be happy, healthy, and productive:

- Keep chicks separate from older birds, apart from the mothering hen.
- If you purchased chicks from different places, make sure to raise them separately just in case there is a problem with one batch.
- Always wash your hands and keep the brooder, water and food stations clean at all times.
- If you also have older birds, don't interchange their feed and water containers with the feed and water containers of your chicks.
- Check up on your chicks on a daily basis and isolate any chick that shows signs of illness.

2. *Feeding Your Chicks*

Once hatched, chicks do not need food straight away. This is what makes it possible to have chicks shipped by mail. However, it is nevertheless a good idea to offer them feed and water as soon as they start moving around. Starter feed is usually finely grounded. Provided it is finely grounded, you won't need to supply any grit that helps them digest the food. You can alternatively purchase baby chick grit from feed stores should your starter feet not be finely grounded.

When providing the chicks with starter feed and water, make sure that they can reach it. Use shallow containers or dishes at the beginning. As the chicks get taller, their feeding containers should also slowly get taller. Other materials which can be used as feeders include the lid of containers, the tops of egg cartons, or paper plates. Meat chicks need to have a full feeder at all times. With all other chicks, it is fine to leave the feeder empty for a few hours.

It is also important to provide a constant supply of clean water. Make sure that the water container is reachable and shallow. Keep the water source as far away from the heat source as possible as chicks prefer to drink cool water. should your chicks appear weak, you can also add a teaspoon of sugar per quart of water to their drinking station to energize them a little.

Lastly, it is very important to keep the feeding and drinking stations clean at all times. Should any spillages occur, make sure to replace the bedding to avoid moisture build-up.

3. _Watching Your Chicks Grow_

With the correct diet, care and warmth, baby chicks will grow quickly. It is important to not mix your young chicks with your older birds until they are fully mature, at around six months, as this will otherwise expose them to bullying and potentially even harm them.

After One Month

Chicks will generally need to be kept in the brooder for around one month. Some slow-growing breeds may need to be kept inside the brooder for longer especially if the weather is still cold or if they do not appear to be well feathered yet.

At the age of about one month, chicks should be moved to a chicken-growing area. If outside temperatures are below 50 degrees °F, the chicks will still need their brooder lamp. At this age, you should also provide your chick with a minimum of 2 square meter per chick. Provided they are well protected form predators and the weather is mild and dry, you can slowly start letting them roam around outside. Also make sure to provide them with a taller feed and drink station and to make sure to provide plenty of water especially as the weather gets warmer.

Most chicks will start roosting as soon as they are feathered. It is therefore important to provide a roost in the chicken-growing area.

Week 6 Until Maturity

When your chicks reach the age of 6 weeks, it is time to change their feed. Broiler chicks should be placed on 'grower rations' or 'finishing rations' with 20% of protein (see *Section 7*). Don't wait to long until you butcher your broiler birds which should be butchered roughly in the 15th week.

Your layers or your other chicks should be placed on 'growing rations' at week 6 which contain 16% protein as well as other vitamins and minerals. At week 18 or when they start laying eggs, layers should be switched to 'layer rations'.

Week 18 – 25: Young Adulthood

Depending on the breed, chickens will reach full maturity sometime between week 18 and week 25. It is wise to put in nesting boxes in week 17 or 18 as this tends to encourage egg-laying. The first few eggs will be small and will often have an odd shape. This is no cause of concern - the eggs should start looking normal after one or two weeks. At this point, your young chickens can also be moved to their coop. If you have older birds, make sure to **gradually** introduce the younger birds to the older birds. This is crucial so as to avoid any bullying or pecking. If you let your birds free-roam, then this is a good time to introduce new birds to your flock.

Section 9: Preventing and Controlling Pests

In this chapter we will discuss the preventative measures you can take to keep your flock pest-free and how to deal with an already established pest population.

1. *Preventing Pests*

Pests do not directly harm your chickens but instead eat up chicken feed and eggs, thereby costing you money. Because of this, it is worth investing your time and a little bit of money in preventing pests from occurring in the first place. After all, this is significantly easier than dealing with an established pest population.

The following is a list of things which you can do in order to prevent pests:

- **Storing your chicken feed appropriately:** Especially if you leave your chicken feed out all the time, it is recommended to store it in mouse and insect-proof containers.
- **Clean feeding areas regularly and keep them dry at all times:** In order to prevent pests, it is important to keep your flock's feeding area clean and dry.
- **Cover feeding and water stations:** This is so to prevent bird droppings from getting into your feeding areas.

- **Remove any potential hiding places and do not let wild birds nest inside your chicken coop:** Remove any potential hiding places inside which rats and mice can find shelter. Removing any nests of wild birds which you find near your chickens is also important as wild birds can not only bring diseases, but also parasites and lice which can be transferred to your flock.

2. *Dealing with Pests*

If you take the above precautions, your chickens will helpfully remain pest-free. If you do encounter pests however, it is important to know how to control and eventually eliminate them. The first step to controlling and eliminating pests however is to identify the pest. Rodents and insects are the most common pests encountered by backyard chicken-keepers

Mice

Mice do not actually harm your chickens nor do they eat eggs. They do however eat chicken feed, thereby costing you significant amounts of money in the long term.

The following are indications that you may have mice in your chicken area:

- Small oblong droppings that are less than 1/32 inch in diameter
- Nesting out of materials such as shredded paper, fabric or dried plant matter in concealed places
- Tiny entrance holes in floors, walls, and feed bags
- Tracks and runways

To control mice, you can either set up a mice trap or use poison bait. Make sure that any poison is not reachable by children, by your chickens or by any other house pets.

Rats

Rats are generally more destructive than mice. Not only can they eat eggs and baby chicks, they have also been found to feed on adult birds in the dark. The latter is a rather rare occurrence but the risk is certainly there.

The following are indications that you may rats threatening your flock:

- Oblong droppings that are significantly larger than mouse droppings
- Large holes penetrating plastic, cinderblock, wire, wood, and other thick or heavy material
- Large tunnels which appear overnight

To control and eliminate rats, you can place traps near their tracks and runways. Traps are however not as effective as rats are more suspicious of new things and are therefore less likely to be caught in a trap. You can also use poison to eliminate any rats. If you do use poison however, make sure to keep it out of reach of children and pets, and remember to change the poison you use from time to time in order to prevent the build-up of resistant rat populations. To prevent rats from harming your adult chicken during the night, you can install a night light near your coop as this allows your chickens to defend themselves against rats.

Insects

Insects and grain pests attack and eat chicken feed. If you find either of the following in your chicken feed, this is an indication that you have insects attacking your stored feed:

- Tiny worms
- Fine webs or webbing

In order to eliminate this pest, you can freeze the chicken feed for a few days. This should kill off most of the pests. Alternatively, you can use up the remaining feed quickly and subsequently clean and dry out the food container, thereby preventing grain pests in the future. Whichever method you use, it is strongly advised **not** to use any pesticide sprays on your chicken feed as many are highly toxic and can therefore harm your birds.

Section 10: Protecting Your Flock from Predators

Predators are animals that attack, kill and eat chickens. Chickens are most vulnerable to attacks by predators in the winter and spring when food is generally scarce. Nevertheless, it is important to keep chickens safe and protected at all times in order to make sure that they do not fall victim to predators.

The most common chicken predators are:

- Bears
- Cats, especially fisher cats and bobcats
- Chicken crows
- Coyotes
- Easels
- Foxes
- Foxes
- Minks
- Neighbourhood dogs
- Possums
- Raccoons
- Raptors, e.g. eagles, hawks, owls, osprey
- Rats
- Skunks
- Snakes (chicks)

The following are measures you should take in order to protect your flock from potential predators:

- Do not let chickens roam freely in areas with a high predator-presence, or restrict roaming to daytime hours only. Keep your chickens penned in the early morning, late evening, and during the night.
- Provide your flock with a predator-proof shelter, thereby preventing night attacks
- Cover coop windows with strong wire.
- Watch out for dogs and prevent your own dogs from chasing chickens.
- Provide your chickens with robust and high fencing. Install electric fencing to protect your flock against coyotes, dogs, foxes, and raccoons.
- If you let your chickens roam, make sure to pick a dark-colored breed to prevent nighttime attacks from raptors.

It is important to keep in mind that predators often return to a previous food source. If your flock has undergone an attack therefore, it is crucial that they are immediately provided with a safer home.

Andy Jacobson

Section 11: Treating Internal and External Parasites

Parasites are a common problem encountered by many backyard chicken-keepers. In fact, it is difficult to prevent parasites altogether. Traditionally, and unless the situation was more severe, many chicken-keepers would leave parasites untreated and would allow nature to take its normal course. Backyard chicken-keepers today have the choice whether or not to treat parasites. Provided your chickens are acting healthy and remain productive, you might be inclined not to treat your chickens' parasites. If you have a small flock on the other hand, or frequent interaction with your birds, then leaving parasites untreated is not recommended. In this section, we will cover the most common parasites, along with everything you need to know to treat both internal and external parasites.

1. _Internal Parasites_

Internal parasites can be common in backyard chickens. Common internal parasites include worms (roundworms, tapeworms, gapeworms) and Coccidia, which is a microscopic protozoa. Internal parasites become problematic when your flock is stressed, whether that is due to a disease or an unsanitary environment. A severe infestation can even lead to poor growth, poor productivity and even death.

Worms

Chickens that have worms are sometimes asymptomatic. Sometimes they may appear thin or unhealthy. Veterinarians can also examine the droppings of chickens in order to determine whether or not they have worms. In general, when treating your flock for worms, you will treat the entire flock. Many backyard chicken-keepers prefer to worm their flock twice a year as a routine preventative procedure. Generally, however, if your flock appears happy, healthy and active, there is usually no need to do so. In the same time, if your flock appears less healthy and exhibit signs of weakness or tiredness, it's probably a good time to get a check-up. If you are raising meat birds, make sure to follow the directions on the label regarding how long to keep your birds before butchering them.

Roundworms

- **What You Need to Know:** Roundworms are a common internal parasite encountered by backyard chickens. They are particularly common among free-range chickens because they can be picked up from the ground as the chickens forage. Heavy infestation with round worms can lead to diarrhea and general weakness. Birds with roundworms will often appear thin with poor feather quality. At other times however, it causes no symptoms. The worms are white and around 3 inches long. They often pass into the feces of the chickens and can easily be spotted this way.

- **Treatment:** Roundworms can be treated using over-the-counter medication that contains piperazine. The medication can be added to the chickens' drinking water. It is advised to treat your chickens as soon as you spot worms in their feces. Many people treat their flock for worms on a regular basis, roughly twice a year in order to avoid a build-up.

Tapeworms

- **What You Need to Know:** Tapeworms are also common in chickens. Tapeworm larvae can be carried by an intermediate, such as an earthworm, snail, slug, termite, which the chicken pick up from the ground. When the chicken gets infested by tapeworms as they eat the host, the parasite attaches itself to the wall of the chicken's intestine. Small portions of the parasite sometimes break off and are passed out in the chicken feces where they can be spotted as small flat pieces that are white and move.

- **Treatment:** If you spot tapeworms and want to worm your chickens, it is advised to consult a veterinarian. No specific treatment exists for treating tapeworms in chickens but treatment that is used to treat tapeworms in other animals can be used provided you know the correct dose. Your veterinarian will be able to advise you off the correct dose for your flock.

Gapeworms

- **What You Need to Know:** Gapeworms are most commonly found in free-ranging chickens. These are more serious than roundworms or tapeworms because they attach themselves to the trachea of the chicken, thereby interfering with breathing. Just like tapeworms, gapeworms enter the chicken's body through an intermediate host which is consumed by the chicken. Chickens infested with gapeworms will breath with their beaks open and often also make grunting sounds, associated with increased work of breathing.

- **Treatment:** There is no specific treatment for gapeworms in backyard chickens. It is thus advised to consult a veterinarian as they can point you toward the right dosage for treatment unspecific to backyard chickens.

Coccidiosis

- **What You Need to Know:** Coccidioa are internal parasites that line the chickens' intestinal wall. Infestation with coccidioa can result in bleeding, which is caused by damage in the intestinal wall. Infestation can also lead to problems related to the absorption of food. The greater the number of parasites in the intestinal tract, the more severe the coccidiosis (the disease caused by coccidioa). Coccidioa is most problematic in younger birds as older birds commonly develop some resistance to the parasite despite still being carriers. Young chickens with heavy infestations often die. Chicks that are under 3 weeks of age are usually asymptomatic. Chicks between week 3 and week 30 that are infested with coccidioa will often exhibit the following symptoms: poor appetite, dehydration, anemia, paleness, and bloody diarrhea.

- **Treatment:** To prevent infestation with coccidioa, it is advised to feed your baby chicks medicated feed with coccidiostats in their first month. If your older birds are infested, you can also treat them with the same medication.

2. *External Parasites*

External parasites, as the term implies, are creatures found outside of the chicken. External parasites suck blood or feed on the skin or feathers of chickens. Those that suck blood can make your birds anemic and those that eat their feathers are irritating to your flock.

Signs of infestation by external parasites include the following:

- Anemia, i.e. pale combs and wattles
- Birds that generally look unhealthy or sick
- Broken feathers

- Parasites crawling on the coop or on your chickens
- Reddened or sore-looking skin
- Reduced productivity
- Scratching and your birds picking on themselves

Free-range chickens will naturally have dust baths which is essential for the health of your flock. The dust removes dirt or dead skin, thereby dislodging and parasites and cleaning the body of any dust that some parasites feed on. If your chickens aren't free range, you can provide them with a deep sand box inside which they can roll around. The size of the box will vary depending on the size of your flock but should generally be at least 12 inches deep and should be no smaller than 15 x 24 inches in size.

Fowl Ticks

- **What You Need to Know:** Ticks are rare in cold areas. A tick infestation however can cause severe illnesses and even death among backyard chickens. They can cause weakness, anemia, weight loss and decreased productivity. Ticks feed at night and are therefore rarely if ever seen. If you suspect ticks, the best way is thus to examine your flock during the night using a light. Fowl ticks feed on the blood of chicken and are large and very visible when filled with blood.

- **Treatment:** Ticks are difficult to control and it is therefore always recommended to consult a veterinarian as to the best tick control products for your specific flock. In order to remove ticks, you will not have to treat your chickens, but their surrounding - the coop and the pasture.

Lice

- **What You Need to Know:** Lice that get on chicken eat their feathers and breakdown their skin. They are small insects that which you can see on your chicken's body if there are many of them. The insect eggs are small dots which you can find glued on your chickens' feathers.

- **Treatment:** To treat lice, you can can use specific insecticides for lice such as carbaryl dust, permethrin and natural pyrethrum on your chickens. There is no need to treat the environment. It is advised to always consult a veterinarian as to the correct way to use the treatment on your chickens.

Mites

- **What You Need to Know:** Mites are tiny insects that are not visible to the eye. They feed on the blood of your flock. They can also bite humans but generally prefer chicken blood. Some mites stay on your chicken's body while others feed at night and hide somewhere in the vicinity during the day. A heavy infestation with mites can be fatal for your chickens. Among other things, they can cause anemia, skin damage, decreased productivity and some even affect bodily organs.

The following are the three types of mites that are most common among backyard chickens:

- **Common Chicken mite**: This type of mite feed on chickens during the night and hides during the day.
- **Northern Fowl mite:** This type of mite causes anemia, scabby skin and a general sense of discomfort to your flock.
- **Scaly Leg mite:** This type of mite infests the legs of chickens

- **Treatment:** In the presence of mites, both your flock as well as their premises must be treated. There are a number of treatments that exist, such as permithrin. For Scaly Leg mites, mineral oil, petroleum jelly or linseed oil can be applied to the legs of your chickens. It is advised to consult a veterinarian as to the type and dosage of treatment to be given.

From the above it is clear that there are numerous parasites that can come into contact with your flock. In smaller flocks particularly, it is difficult to prevent infestation with parasites. Whether you have a small or a big flock, it is important to check your flock for parasites from regularly. Early detection and preventative treatment can avoid unfavorable consequences in the long-term, such as a flock outbreak.

Section 12: Last but Not Least

I would like to take this opportunity to thank you for purchasing this book. I hope you now have a solid foundation on the process, and that you are equipped with the knowledge to put you on the path to raising chickens in your very own backyard!

My final piece of advice - no matter how diligent you are in your research, your best learning will come from getting started and getting to know and understand your flock.

I sincerely wish you the best of luck in your chicken raising journey!

Best wishes,

Andy Jacobson

Bonus: The Essential Chicken Coops Guide: A Step-By-Step Guide to Planning and Building Your Own Chicken Coop

Foreword

The benefits of raising your own chickens are countless - from having an abundance of fresh and nutritious eggs, to giving yourself a strong feeling of self-sufficiency. No matter what your motivation is for raising chickens, you will need to provide them with a suitable housing arrangement! As I'm sure you already know, there is the option to purchase pre-made chicken coops, but there's no reason to pay for something that you can create yourself! Building your own chicken coop can be a straightforward process with the correct guidance. So why not take your self-sufficiency to the next level?

There is a lot of mismatched information spread around which can often make it extremely confusing when it comes to figuring out how to start building your coop. To relieve this frustration, this guide will give you the proven easy-to-follow methods which will make the building process a breeze, even if your DIY skills are basic. You will quickly learn all the requirements for a chicken coop, and then soon be on your way to constructing your very own chicken coop by following the construction guidelines that are provided. I've been mindful to ensure that everything is covered in a manageable amount of detail which will prevent any frustration when you start the process of bringing your chicken chalet to life!

This is the 'go to' guide for building sustainable chicken coops that covers the following: Chicken Coop Foundations, Equipment, Tools, and Materials, The Coop Building Process, Adding the Extras, This will serve as a valuable resource to continuously revisit as you develop and improve your coops.

If you are completely new to self-built chicken coops, I suggest reading the books in the order it has been structured with. If not, and you're either looking for a refresher or information on a specific topic, go right ahead to the sections that are most relevant to your building goals.

Best wishes,

Andy Jacobson

Section 1: The Foundations of Chicken Coops

Chicken Housing Basics

A chicken coop provides the crucial shelter that your chickens require. Chicken coops can be large in size and elaborate, small and basic, or a combination of both. That said, the right coop for you solely depends on a variety of factors: the amount of chickens you plan to keep, your available space, weather, and also any predators that could pose a threat to your flock.

Let's start with an overview of the fundamentals that you will need to consider before planning and building your coop.

Shelter and protection: Your coop will need to protect your chickens from any harsh weather. On top of this, your flock will need to be safeguarded from any predatory animals. The is by far the main and most important purpose of your coop.

Adequate space: As a general rule of thumb, you should allow 2 - 4 square feet of floor space for each chicken you have.

Keeping the coop clean: Expect your coop to get dirty and develop some bad smells. To counter this, you will want to make sure that there is adequate ventilation to rid smells. You should also have an efficient cleaning routine in place to maintain the coop.

Lighting: It is crucial that your chickens get an adequate amount of sunlight. Lighting is therefore an important consideration.

Temperature: Chickens tend to be happiest at temperatures between 45 to 85 degrees Fahrenheit.

Chicken Coop Features

Although there is a lot of scope for experimentation and adding personal touches to your chicken coop, there are some fundamental features that your coop must have.

Roosts:

Your chickens need somewhere to sleep, and this is what the 'roost' is for. In the wild, chickens have evolved to sleep on sheltered branches that offer them protection from the weather and predators. The roost serves as an elevated area that replicates this sleeping process for your chickens. Each bird should have around 12 inches of roost and the roost needs to be positioned higher than the nesting boxes and away from drafty spots. A ramp can be used to help chickens reach the roost.

Nest boxes:

Nest boxes are where your hens lay their eggs - these are separate areas that are important if you want to encourage the production of eggs. Theses boxes are usually shared by hens and each box should be at least 12 square inches, warm, and be elevated 3 to 4 feet of the floor.

Chicken runs:

A chicken run is the open space where your flock can freely move around as well as get access to sunshine and air. This area is most commonly enclosed by wire mesh fencing. The bigger this area is, the better! Having a large chicken run plays a central role in the general well-being of your flock.

Ramps:

As chickens are not the best flyers, it is important to provide them with ramps for them to get in and out of the coop with ease.

Placing Your Coop and Its Size:

It's very important to choose a suitable location for your coop, and there are a number of factors that should be considered for this. Firstly, you need to make sure that you are legally allowed to have a coop in your yard. I recommend getting approval from your local authorities - the last thing you want is to build a beautiful coop and then start getting complaints and notices to remove it!

Proximity:

You don't want your coop to be too far away from your house, which will make it more challenging each time you need to go and check up on your flock. This is also likely to make them more susceptible to predatory animals. It's best to build the coop within a fairly close proximity to your house which will allow you to easily see it. That said, it's not a good idea to have the coop too close to your house either as they can be noisy at times.

Water supply:

On top of cleaning the coop regularly, you will also need to constantly provide fresh water for your chickens. Keep this in mind and make sure your coop is located within reach of a watering hose – this will save you a lot of work lugging buckets of water back and forth.

Drainage:

Water drainage is another key consideration. If your coop is placed in an area that is depressed (e.g. bottom of a slope) it will be likely to generate a build up of water when it rains. Try to locate your coop in an even area that will have a good amount of drainage.

Coop Sizing:

The size of your coop will depend upon how much space you have available, and this will ultimately determine the size of the flock that you can keep. There should be around 2 to 4 sq. ft. of floor area for each chicken in the coop, and at least 4 sq. ft. of area in the outdoor run. Be sure to carefully consider this when deciding on the size of your flock.

Choosing Your Style of Coop:

Firstly, when planning what type of coop to build, it's equally important to think about aesthetics. How do you want your coop to look? Start thinking about what will look best in your yard. The style of your coop will of course depend on the level of your carpentry skills - if you have basic DIY skills it will be best to start with a coop that is smaller with a simple design. We will be going through coop building guidelines later on, but for now it's time to cover some of the common coop types.

'A Frames' and Hoops:

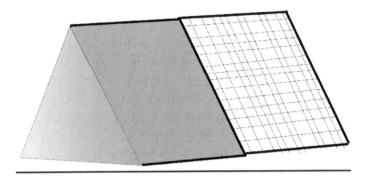

These coop types are among the most basic designs for coops, but are great if you only have a small area available and plan on keeping a small flock. They are very affordable and only require few tools and materials. 'A frames' have a triangular shape that is made from two sides that lean in against each other. This is usually connected to a run area that is exactly the same shape.

Hoop coops are similar in layout but instead of triangular they are round in shape. Hoop coops are usually made from flexible PVC piping with fencing and fabric covering the exterior.

Tractor Coops:

Coops can be built in a way that allows for easy transportation between different locations. Tractor coops have walls and roofs, but they don't have flooring. The ground of the yard provides the flooring for the flock wherever the coop is placed. They are called tractors because they are fitted with wheels which allows them to be easily moved around.

The All In One Coop:

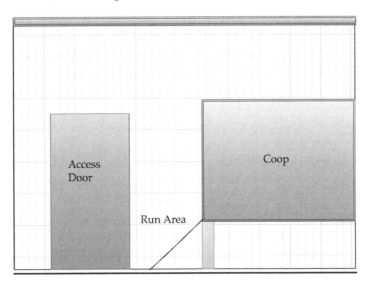

All in one coops are designed to have the coop and run all under one roof. This roof is generally large enough for you to physically enter the run which facilitates the maintenance of your flock. As you can imagine, this style of coop is usually significantly large than the 'A frame' coops or hoop frame coops. The all in one coop has a large solid structure which requires a longer building process.

The Walk In Coop:

This is the most sophisticated type of coop which will require the most space and is also the costliest and most laborious to construct. Think of this as the top of the range 'premium' coop.

On the upside, being able to physically enter your coop will make maintaining your flock significantly more efficient - you can easily gain access to all areas of your coop, which makes the upkeep of your coop much easier than with smaller and more basic designs. The other benefit is that you can keep a much larger flock. The run is usually constructed separately which will also take up a considerable amount of space.

As mentioned previously, I always recommend starting with a simple and basic coop. With time and once you're ready to make the financial investment, you can eventually upsize to a walk in coop.

Section 2: Equipment, Tools, and Materials

Whatever coop you decide on building, you will need the correct tolls and materials to bring your dream coop to life. The great thing is you definitely don't need an arsenal of premium specialist equipment, but a selection of fairly basic tools will suffice when it comes to building your coop. This section will cover the tools that you will need to have on site so you're completely ready when the building begins!

Safety First

To keep yourself out of harm's way, I strongly suggest having the following 3 safety essentials on hand for any coop build.

- **Safety goggles**
- **Earplugs**
- **Safety gloves**

You might also want to wear a tool belt to ensure any other tools are easily accessible when you need them.

Garden Tools

If the location of your coop requires some clearing before building, I suggest having the following tools ready for preparing the location.

- **Rake**
- **Shovel**

- **Mattock**

Other Tools and Equipment

Here is a summary of the other tools and equipment you will need, depending on the type of coop you decide on building.

- **Measuring tools:** This almost goes without saying, but you will definitely need a measuring tape and and pencil to make sure everything is accurately cut.
- **Saw:** You will need to be able to efficiently cut wood, so make sure you have a saw that you are comfortable using.
- **Posthole digger or Power Auger:** Depending on your plans, it is a possibility that you will need to dig some postholes.
- **Wire working tools:** You will be working with mesh made from wire which will be on the exterior of your chicken run, and possibly on some areas of your coop. Make sure you have an effective wire cutting tool for this.
- **Hammer**
- **Screwdriver**
- **Drill**
- **Level and Square**

These are pretty much all the main tools that you will need. You might wish to utilize a variety of other tools to help you at certain parts of the process, but this depends on your preferences and building style.

Materials

The coop building guidelines later on in this guide will list the exact materials you will need for each plan, but below you can find the essential materials that you will require.

Board lumber: The framework of your coop will be made of board lumber. The most common are 2 x 4 and 2 x 3 (thickness x width) - you may need some other sizes depending on your plan.

Sheet lumber: This wood is used on the very outer layer of your coop.

Nails and screws: To fasten parts together – nails and screws are crucial for keeping your coop standing up! You can use either nails, screws, or a combination of both. This ultimately comes down to personal preference.

Flooring: The flooring in a coop is generally made from plywood, or another type of sheet wood. On top of this, it's important to think about what will make ongoing maintenance efficient. I recommend using lino flooring with a loose material on top of the sheet wood flooring. This will make cleaning easiest. Some may wish to use a dirt or concrete floor - again, this comes down to your available space and preference.

Plywood for walls: There are plenty of materials that you can use for the walls of the coop, but I generally recommend thick plywood as the most effective material.

Roofing materials: The roofing is a crucial component of the coop as this serves the main function of protecting your flock. Most coops are constructed using multiple overlapping layers. You can choose between shingles and other corrugated material which work well with rainfall. Underneath the outermost layer, you will need to place tar paper or felt which acts as a moisture barrier.

Wire mesh: Along with materials to build your coop, you will also need materials to build the run for your coop. Wire mesh is a key material to enclose your chicken run.

Supporting posts: You will also need wooden posts that the wire mesh can be wrapped around to support the run. The most commonly used is a 4 x 4 post.

Recycled Material

To promote greater self-sufficiency, I suggest recycling any existing material that you may have access to. This is an excellent way to reduce the cost of building your coop - I also find it more satisfying as your coop feels all the more 'home-made'.

Start thinking about where you can source these materials so that they can be easily obtained when you reach the building instructions provided later on in the book.

Quantity of Materials

Once you have made your plan for your coop, I recommend dividing this into separate sections and list the types of wood and materials that you will need for each. You can then add this together to make sure that you source the correct amounts. I always recommend buying/sourcing slightly more than you have predicted - this will give you some flexibility as well as allow for any accidental measuring errors!

Section 3: Building the Coop

The construction process of your chicken coop takes some time and dedication, and I encourage you to take your time in order to create something that will satisfy for the long-term. One important consideration for the building process is to think about when you will actually need it. You should aim to have your coop fully constructed well in advance of when your chicks are ready to be placed into their new home.

In this section we will cover the ins and outs of building your coop, from site preparation, to adding the floor, walls, and roof.

The Ideal Location - Preparing Your Coop Site

You have the choice to place your coop in a variety of areas, and ideally this will be in a clear area that has enough space to cater for the coop. In most cases though there will be some clearing to do - and this is the starting point to creating a great coop space. We will now be covering how you can best prepare your site before starting your construction.

Site Clearance

Ideally, you will want to create a bare area of ground for your site, and these are the preliminary tasks you will need to complete on your site:

- Clear any leaves or debris
- Clear any plants
- Remove any other potential interferences

Ground Level:

In order for your coop to stand straight, you will of course need to make sure that the ground beneath it is even. I recommend using a high quality line level - you can dig two stakes into the ground and attach string between them, and then use a line level to gauge how even the ground is.

Using Posts:

If your site is not level, or you want to have an elevated coop, you have the option to install posts into the ground - these will act as vertical supports for the coop. This can be achieved by inserting a wooden post into a concrete bed which sits above the gravel. The hole for the wooden post can be created using either a posthole digger or a power auger.

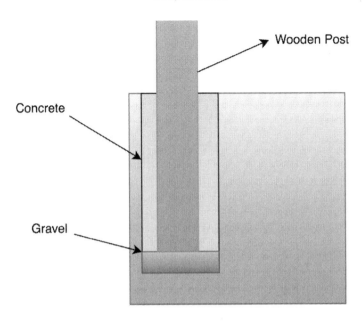

The Framing

Think of the frame as the 'skeleton' for your coop -
everything else is built around it. The frame therefore plays
a key role in determining the lifespan of the coop. A robust
frame requires a roof, walls, and a floor. I recommend using
2 x 4 framing. The floor framing acts as a support for the
material that you will use as the flooring. The wall framing
will give stiffness to the walls and the roof framing will act
as a support for the roofing material.

Building the Floor:

If your coop is smaller and not designed for you to
physically enter it (e.g. 'A frame' coop or hoop coop), you
will not need super duty flooring. On the other hand, if you

are planning on building a larger walk-in coop, you will need a heavy duty floor that is supported by a 'subfloor' that is made up of joists. The subfloor is essentially a box shaped support made out of joists that will sit under the flooring that you choose.

The decking will sit on top of the subfloor - this should be made of approximately 3/4 inch plywood.

Walls: No matter what type of chicken coop you decide to build; it will definitely need some reliable walls. For smaller and more basic coops, the wall structure can be simplistic, but for larger walk in coops, they will need to be structurally robust. Walls are made up of 'studs' that fit into the bottom flooring plates and the top roofing plates. The studs will have to account for the entry door and for any windows.

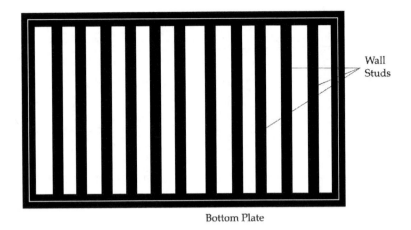

Wall
Studs

Bottom Plate

One you have figured out the placement of your studs in relation to the bottom and top plates, use reliable fasteners (nails/screws) to assemble the studs to the plates. I recommend using plywood to build strong and long-lasting exterior walls onto your frame of studs.

Doors and windows: An efficient entry to the coop is essential - a door can be added in a variety of ways which depends on your personal preferences. Like doors, there are many different ways in which you can add windows to your coop. This can be done using a simple mesh opening, or a more sophisticated hatch that can be latched closed. Extra framing is needed to provide ample support for any coop doors and windows. Once you have taken measurements for your doors and windows, they will need to be built in the same way you built the entire wall frame with studs.

Once all wall frames have been erected, these can be fastened to the subfloor and then attached to the other wall frames.

Roofing: Things can get slightly more challenging when it comes to building a roof for your coop. But don't be discouraged – building the roof should still be perfectly manageable if you've been able to construct the flooring and walls successfully! The great thing is that it can be as simple or as complicated as you want it to be. For the most basic type of roof, a 'shed roof' can be built which is essentially a flat surface across the top of the coop which is elevated slightly at one end. The roof should be elevated at a 'pitch' of 20 to 40 degrees to allow for rain drainage. Alternatively, you can opt for a more traditional ('gable') triangular roof with two sloping sides that meet at the top.

Much like the other structural elements that make up the coop, the roof requires a support frame. On a gable roof, joists are placed horizontally and are fastened together at the top of the 'A' point.

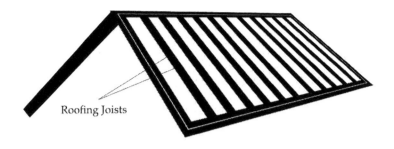

Roofing Joists

One you have contracted the frame for your roof, you can use rafter ties to securely fasten the frame to the top plate of the walls.

Installing the Outer-Frame Parts

Once you reach this stage, your coop should be starting to take good shape! Sitting on outside of the frame will be the exterior surfaces that enclose the whole coop:

Placing the walls: I recommend using readily available plywood. This can be easily fastened to the exterior of the stud frame.

Placing the doors and hatch: A basic door frame can be constructed and added to to the coop using door hinges. The same goes for any hatches that you would like to add.

Windows: Windows play an important role in the well-being of your flock by providing them with much appreciated light. Similar to the door frame, you can create a solid panel and hardware that will allow the window to be open and closed. You can then add wire mesh to the inside to enclose the coop. Remember, there's no set way to add windows, so this is a great opportunity to let your creativity shine! As long as the window serves its purpose and you are satisfied with it, then all is well!

Finishing off the roof: I recommend using asphalt shingles in order to provide a waterproof shelter for your coop. This creates a multi-layered roof that is both robust and moisture-resistant. This type of roof is seen on many homes for good reason – it is a very efficient roofing system. The installation involves multiple stages: laying down sheathing, fascia boards and underlayment, and then placing multiple shingles. Another alternative option for roofing is using corrugated panels.

Air vents: this can be achieved in a variety of ways, for example through using wall vents and ridge vents - you just need to make sure that air can freely circulate in your coop.

Section 4: Adding the Extras: Roosts, Nest Boxes, Ramps, and Runs

Once you have erected the main exterior build of your coop, it's time to start thinking about adding all the essential features inside of the coop.

Finishing the flooring:

Before anything else, I strongly recommend laying out linoleum or vinyl flooring which will make things significantly easier when it comes to cleaning. Cut this to the correct size and use adhesive or wide headed nails to affix to the floor.

Roosts:

As mentioned earlier, chickens prefer to sleep in a place that is elevated from the ground, so we need to provide an area that satisfies this. Each chicken will need around 12 inches of roost space, and they prefer this space to be as high as possible within the coop. Always keep in mind that your flock will create dropping that will end up directly beneath the roost, so be sure to keep this area clear of any feed or water.

I recommend building a roost that is like a step ladder - this will give multiple birds places to roost, all whilst making the best use of the space available.

Nest boxes:

The next box is crucial if you want to maximize egg production, and I don't see why you wouldn't! Here are some considerations you should make when designing and building nest boxes.

Size - A good minimum size for a nest box is 12 inches by 12 inches. You can have them larger than this, but I wouldn't recommend this as it could lead to having too many hens in one nest at a time - this can result in a number of broken eggs!

How many? - You don't need to have the same amount of nest boxes as you have hens - they will use them in turn, so there's no need to use up more space than necessary.

Location? - Hens prefer to be closely located to one another, so be sure to place all nest boxed next to each other. In addition to this, try to place them in the darkest and warmest corner of the coop.

Making the nest boxes comfortable - Use loose straw or hay to line the nest boxes - your hens will love this!

In order to build the nest boxes, you can use extra bits of wood to construct a frame, and enclose the frame with plywood. Leave one side open to allow your hens to enter the box. Finally, add a hatch for easy access. Another viable option is to buy pre-fabricated nest boxes which can make things slightly easier when it comes to cleaning.

Ramps:

If you have a coop with a door that is located off the ground, you will also need to create a basic ramp to ensure your flock can get in and out of the coop easily. This can be as simple as adding an extra piece of wooden scrap with some rungs attached to it to help the birds with grip.

Setting up the Chicken Run

Although we have covered the ins and outs of constructing the main section of the coop, we are yet to start considering what makes an effective run space. The run is to be placed on the outside of the coop. Chickens require a good amount of time outside, so it's our duty to provide them with a safe area to catch some sunrays and get fresh air. For many coops such as the 'A-frame' coop, hoop coop or all-in-one coop, the run can be directly attached to the main coop body. But even with these coops, you may wish to provide a larger space for your flock to run around.

A run should provide around 6 square feet for each bird in

your flock, but no harm is done by having more than this. Ideally, you should construct the run so it is directly attached to the main coop. This allows your flock to freely come and go as they please.

To build the chicken run, follow the steps below:

1. **Plan the layout and size of the run:** This will depend on your space available and the size of your flock.
2. **Place fence posts in each corner.**
3. **Size, measure and cut wire mesh:** Ensure that this is strong enough to guard your flock from any potential predators.
4. **Fasten the wire mesh to the framing of the run:** Do this securely using heavy duty staples and/or screws and washers.

Providing Electricity for Your Coop:

Having electricity access for your coop may seem like an unnecessary luxury to some, but this will not only be helpful in terms of providing you with lighting whilst doing maintenance - it will also help your chickens lay eggs. On top of this, this will also help keep your coop heated in the winter which will significantly improve the well-being of your flock. Providing electricity can be achieved in a number of ways, and will mostly depend on where your coop is situated. If necessary, invest in a professional to come in and install a weatherproof electricity supply. This investment will pay for itself in the long term!

Section 5: Coop Plan 1 - The Minimalist Coop

Now that you have an overview of everything that needs to be considered to build an effective coop for your flock, I will now share with you some actual coop plans that you can build yourself. These plan will outline all the materials that you will need to source, along with the steps to take to construct the coop.

Choose a plan that is best suited to your needs and available space and use the steps as a guideline to bring your coop to life. Although these are set plans, there is still room for improvisation and for you to add some flair and uniqueness to the designs where you see fit. This is one of my favorite parts of the process - being able to make the coop truly your own creation! I encourage you to plan out a reasonable timeline and set goals which will help you stay on track.

The Minimalist Coop

This is a 'back-to-basics' coop that doesn't require studs in the wall frame which makes it a great starter coop for you to build. This is a straightforward design that can be built within a day! Expect to spend up to $200-250 on materials.

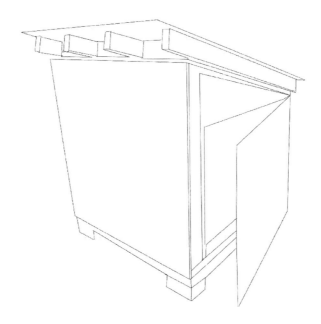

The minimalist coop is a simple 4 foot by 4 foot by 4 foot cube which is suitable for up to 5 birds. One wall has an integrated hinge door for easy access, and you can fit up to 3 nest boxes inside the coop. Don't forget to erect a run on the exterior of the coop.

List of Materials

Here is a summary of the materials you will need - feel free to make changes to the materials as you see fit for your requirements and preferences.

Wood:

- 1 x 4 by 8 inches sheet of 5/8 inches oriented strand board
- 2 x 4 by 8 inches sheet of 5/8 plywood
- 2 x 8 inch of 4 by 4 of lumber (pressure treated)
- 13 8 inch lengths of 2 by 4 lumber

Hardware:

- 4 pier blocks (concrete)
- Corrugated roof panels to cover 48 by 64 inches
- A lock (preferably chain)
- 12 rafter ties
- 2 pieces of 12 by 48 inches wire mesh
- Various fasteners (nails and screws)

Use the following steps as a guideline for constructing the coop:

1. **Build the floor:** Attach the floor joists to assemble a subfloor frame following the same guidelines as outlined in section 3. Place the strand board on top of this to form the main decking. The flooring system should be placed above the pier blocks.
2. **Walls:** Construct framing for all walls and fasten these together.
3. **Roof:** Construct the roof framing using the rafters and rafter ties.
4. **Construct the nest boxes:** You can construct the next boxes using spare plywood. The box size will depend on your preferences – just make sure they meet the minimum requirements as outlined in section 3.
5. **Adding the exterior:** Fasten plywood to all walls and create the door on one side wall using hinges.

6. **Fasten the wire mesh:** This can be fastened over any open areas on the coop.
7. **Place the roofing:** Use the corrugated panels to create secure roofing for the coop.

There you have it! Again, there is a lot of scope for creativity to built this coop exactly how you see fit for your requirements - happy building!

Section 6: Coop Plan 2 - The 'A Frame'

As mentioned earlier in the book, the 'A frame' is another great basic coop that is used by many chicken owners. It's a great coop for those with limited space, and although it is generally used with smaller flocks, this design can be scaled up to meet your needs. This is my number one recommendation for a first time coop builder.

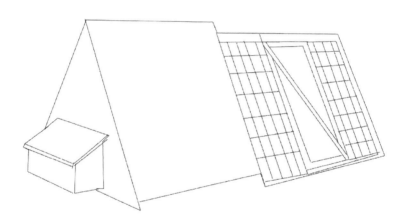

This plan is designed to be around 4 feet wide and 10 feet long, which will make it a perfect coop for a flock of up to 4 chickens. The access door is one complete side of the coop, which gives you easy access for maintenance. There is another chicken door on the side that your flock can use to enter the run. I recommend building just 2 nest boxes for this modest sized coop. The run sits directly adjacent to the coop which your birds will love! In terms of costs, you can expect to spend under $275 for all materials.

List of Materials

Here is a summary of the materials you will need - feel free to make changes to the materials as you see fit for your requirements and preferences.

Wood:

- 3 x 4 by 8 inches T1-11 sheets
- 1 x 4 by 4 sheet of 1/16 inch oriented strand board
- 3 x (4 inch length 2 by 4 inch lumber, pressure treated)
- 3 x (6 inch length 2 by 3 inch lumber, pressure treated)
- 18 x (6 inch length 2 by 3 inch lumber)
- 1 x 4 inch length 2 by 2 inch lumber
- 2 x (6 inch length 1 by 3 inch lumber, pressure treated)
- 2 x (6 inch length 1 by 3 inch lumber)
- 1 x (8 inch length 1 by 2 inch lumber)

Hardware:

- Wire mesh
- Metal sheet
- Hinges, T style
- Eye latches
- Gate latch

Use the following steps as a guideline for constructing the coop:

Build the shelter: Start with the main shelter of the coop which is the main 'A frame". Create the main door using hinges.

Build the next boxes: Use spare plywood.

Create the roost: As discussed earlier in the book, there are many designs and ways in which you can build the roost. Just make sure it's positioned in a space which is higher than the nesting boxes and away from drafty spots.

Construct the run: Build a secure run according to your preferences and securely fasten this to the side of the coop.

Conclusion: Last but Not Least

I would like to take this opportunity to thank you for downloading this book. I hope you now have a solid foundation on what you need to create a brilliant coop, and how you can start making your coop vision a reality!

My final piece of advice - no matter how diligent you are in your research and planning, your best learning will come from *doing,* so don't hesitate in getting started. Start simple, perhaps with one of the basic coops. Once you put your knowledge into practice you'll soon have the skills to advance onto more challenging coop designs, and perhaps increase your flock as well.

I sincerely wish you the best of luck in your coop-building venture!

Best wishes,

Andy Jacobson

Made in the USA
Lexington, KY
15 March 2018